WHAT DOES
THIS SAY?

Bil Keane

FAWCETT GOLD MEDAL • NEW YORK

A Fawcett Gold Medal Book
Published by Ballantine Books
Copyright © 1994 by Bil Keane, Inc.
Distributed by King Features Syndicate, Inc.

Library of Congress Catalog Card Number: 94-94205

ISBN 0-449-14814-9

Printed in Canada

First Edition: September 1994

10 9 8 7 6 5

"PJ started eating his cupcake
before I could peel the
skin off it."

"PJ isn't an angel. Angels
are invisible."

"When there's only half a moon,
where does the other half go?"

"This is money, PJ. It's what a
lot of grownups fight about."

"Billy's throat doesn't feel
sore to me."

"Big hand's on nine, little hand's on three...No one in the place except you 'n' me..."

"Are the boys allowed on the
new loveseat?"

"Wasn't he on 'America's Most Wanted' last week?"

"I don't wanna be a king if they
hafta eat blackbird pies."

"Are you allowed to draw hair
with a bald point pen?"

"Stop fighting! I'm EVERY-BODY'S Valentine!"

"I'm only seven years old
and already I'm tired
of commercials."

"Mommy! Here's the upscalator!"

"Daddy, have you seen a jar with
my bug collection in it?"

"When we have children Mommy will be promoted to Grandma."

"Are the Grammy Awards for the
best grandmothers?"

"When I grow up do I hafta be
called a dult?"

"'Giddyap' means 'go' in cowboy."

"Billy gave me fifteen pennies
and I only had to give him
one quarter!"

"Mommy, do we have any pretzels?"

"Is there a spelling Hall of Fame?"

"Bear claws? Yeeulk!"

"Mommy, when I grow up will
we be sisters?"

"Can I see my teddy bear's bones?"

"Senior citizens are very OLD
people — like Mommy
and Daddy."

"Bye, Grandma! Thank you for enjoyin' us."

"Jeffy's a speed looker."

"Today's my birthday and I still
look the same."

"The area code is our phone
number's first name."

"Jeffy called me a four-letter
word — SCUD!"

"If I plant this, will a palm
tree grow?"

"There's 15 minutes left, Mommy.
Let's shop some more!"

"Look at all the chicklets!"

"I camouflaged mine so it'll be
hard to find."

"The Easter Bunny doesn't come down the chimney, Jeffy. Don't you know rabbits can't hop all the way up to the roof?"

"The candy's all gone. I'm using
it for my marbles."

"Instead of string beans and
lima beans, couldn't we
have jelly beans?"

"Kittycat has a built-in antenna,
but no radio."

"Mommy, what's cookin' in
that pot?"

"Listen! Isn't that the Ninja
Turtles coming on?"

"Once PJ learns a new word he sure
does practice it a lot."

"Mom! I can't wear THOSE pajamas
during baseball season!"

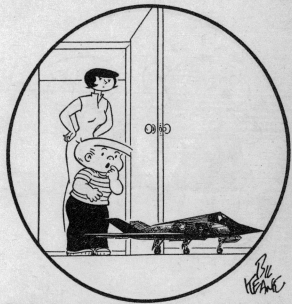

"Pick up WHAT plane? I don't see any plane. I know there's a Stealth plane around here somewhere, but I can't see it!"

"I let Billy have some of my candy
and he took a MEGABITE!"

"Why can't our teachers be like
Alex Trebek and give us all
the answers?"

"It's a foul ball if it goes into the pews."

"He's doin' his income tax
homework."

"...and say hi to our grandfather
who art in heaven, too."

"I'm too tired to go to bed."

"Who colored those bird's
eggs blue?"

"Mommy! Billy's tilting back in
his chair again!"

"Wanna smell my breath, Daddy? I
just ate some peanut butter."

"But, Mom! We're supposed to be
saving water!"

"...happily ever after. And now
you know...the REST of
the story."

"Don't wash this shirt any more,
Mommy. It's getting hard
to read."

"I have a very 'portant paper for you from Miss Johnson. But I left it on the bus."

"Hi, Ricky. Wanna attend the world
premiere of a home video?"

"Granddad can see the OTHER side
of the moon from up in heaven."

"Grandma, who eats all these
cookies when we're not
visitin' you?"

"It's not snow, sweetheart. It's
blossoms from the trees."

"They've got the Red Sea
colored blue!"

"She's a mind reader. She
has ESPN."

"Is this the no-smoking section?"

"We don't say 'CAN I,' Jeffy.
It's 'MAY I' 'cause this
is May."

"Miss Johnson told us a secret. We're
gonna make Mother's Day cards
and we're not to tell anybody."

"Look. Shadowmation."

"Feet aren't fair. The two
littlest piggies are too far
from each other."

"Better start bein' good, Mommy.
Mother's Day is coming soon."

"There's a butterfly all squished
up inside that caterpillar just
waitin' to get out."

"I picked this yellow flower off
our lawn, Mommy! Will you
vase it for me?"

"Gentlemen, start your homework!"

"We got our school pictures!
Want me to autograph
one for you?"

"No trick riding, please."

"I like weeping willows. They have floor-length branches."

"At my uncle's wedding, Dolly was
the flower girl and I was the
ring master."

"Could I have some credit cards
for my purse so I can be like
a REAL woman?"

"They put those wires there to give
the birds a place to sit."

"Gallop, horsey!"

"Know what I like about this suit?
When I spill stuff on it
nobody can tell."

"I feel sorry for Daddy. HIS
vitamin pills don't look
like anybody."

"When the puddles wiggle you
know it's raining."

"That's Tom Cruise. They named the missiles after him."

"Isn't there anything on besides
words and numbers?"

"That must be their bedroom window.
It has a yawning over it."

"It could be worse, Barfy. That's
not a scratching paw."

"I ordered pizza."

"Daddy, can we glue this half a
toothpick to the other half that's
stuck in the keyhole?"

"Mommy said to behave, so I'm
bein' as hayve as I can."

"What are we watchin'? Well, Mommy's watchin' 'Homecoming,' my dad's watchin' 'Cold Fire,' Dolly's watchin' 'Adam Raccoon'..."

"Red Riding was Robin Hood's
little girl."

"You're not foolin' anybody,
Jeffy! Give me back my
play phone."

"Guess what! They want me back
again in September!"

"Oh no! Doesn't God know
school's out?"

"When I grow up I'm gonna be an
intestine on a game show."

"Mommy, are you getting something for Daddy, too, or is he only allowed FOUR things on his Father's Day list?"

"Wake up, Daddy, and see what you got for Father's Day!"

"Mommy, do you have to go to college to be a king?"

"You washed the wag right out
of his tail."

"Please pass the salad lotion."

"They made a lot of my money
disappear."

"Will somebody open up the light
for me, please?"

"These dandelions need a shave!"

"More, Mommy, more. I can still
see the pie."

"Mirrors are there to remind us
what we look like in case
we forget."

"Barfy, you should brush your
nose after eating."

"The picture was so-so, but I'd
give the popcorn two
thumbs up."

"Jack Spratt would eat low fat,
and his wife's cholesterol
was high..."

"Look, the ducks are havin'
a parade!"

"Oh beautiful for spaceship skies..."

"I wish we could push a pause
button and freeze the picture."

"I think I finally got the last
Christmas tree needle."

"God must've stayed up all night to make such a beautiful morning!"

"Your watch isn't in there, Daddy.
We hid it in the sand so nobody
would steal it."

"It's the fourteenth inning, Daddy.
Do we stretch again?"

"Every time I call the operator
she uses a different voice."

"When will my braces come in?"

"Sundials don't need batteries,
Jeffy. They're solar-powered."

"One finger means reach the plate
in one bounce. Two fingers,
two bounces..."

"Because they don't have Concordes
between here and Grandma's,
that's why!"

"Why don't strawberries have
their seeds inside like
other fruits do?"

"Here you go, PJ — the beginner's slope."

"I know we hang our Christmas wreath from that nail, but what's it for in the summer?"

"I'm tellin' Mommy. You're goin'
over her head."

"I didn't hurt your bear when I hit him — he's still smilin'!"

"Every sunset is different, PJ.
They never have reruns."

Call toll free 1-800-733-3000 to order by phone and use your major credit card. Or use this coupon to order by mail.

___ARE YOU AWAKE, DADDY?	449-14809-2	$3.99
___BABY ON BOARD	449-13381-8	$3.50
___CAN I HAVE A COOKIE?	449-12972-1	$3.99
___DADDY'S LITTLE HELPERS	449-13106-8	$3.99
___DOLLY HIT ME BACK!	449-13032-0	$3.99
___ENJOY YOURSELVES!	449-14812-2	$3.99
___FOR THIS I WENT TO COLLEGE?	449-12849-0	$3.99
___GO TO YOUR ROOM!	449-12610-2	$3.99
___GOOD MORNING, SUNSHINE	449-12895-4	$3.99
___GRANDDAD IT'S MORNING!	449-13379-6	$3.50
___GRANDMA WAS HERE	449-12835-0	$3.99
___HE FOLLOWED ME HOME	449-12425-8	$3.99
___HELLO, GRANDMA?	449-12930-6	$3.50
___HOW DO YOU TURN IT ON?	449-12421-5	$3.50
___I CAN'T UNTIE MY SHOES	449-13065-7	$3.95
___I COULD HEAR CHEWING	449-13372-9	$3.50
___I DRESSED MYSELF	449-12931-4	$3.99
___I HAD A FRIGHTMARE!	449-14615-4	$3.99
___I JUST DROPPED GRANDMA!	449-14617-0	$3.50
___I'LL SHOVEL THE CARDS	449-14807-6	$3.99
___I'M ALREADY TUCKED IN	449-13098-3	$3.99
___I'M WEARIN' A ZUCCHINI!	449-14618-9	$3.99
___IT'S MUDDY OUT TODAY	449-13376-1	$3.50
___IT'S MY BIRTHDAY SUIT	449-12420-7	$3.50
___IT'S UP AND LET 'EM AT ME	449-14619-7	$3.50
___JEFFY'S LOOKIN' AT ME	449-12869-5	$3.99
___KITTYCAT'S MOTOR IS RUNNING	449-12422-3	$3.99
___LOOK! A FLUTTERBY!	449-14810-6	$3.99
___LOOK WHO'S HERE	449-13276-5	$3.99
___MINE!	449-13264-1	$3.50
___MY TURN NEXT!	449-12792-3	$3.99
___NOT ME!	449-13405-9	$3.50
___OOPS! WE'RE OUT JUICE!	449-13373-7	$3.50
___PASGHETTI & MEAT BULBS	449-13241-2	$3.50
___PEACE, MOMMY, PEACE	449-13194-7	$3.99
___PEEKABOO! I LOVE YOU!	449-12824-5	$3.99
___PICK UP WHAT THINGS?	449-12785-0	$3.99
___PJ'S STILL HUNGRY	449-13044-0	$3.50
___PJ'S BAREFOOT ALL OVER!	449-14811-4	$3.99
___QUIET! MOMMY'S ASLEEP!	449-12909-8	$3.50
___QUIET, SAM!	449-14616-2	$3.50
___SAM'S TAKIN' A CATNAP!	449-14808-4	$3.99
___THE SKY'S ALL WRINKLED	449-14620-0	$3.99
___SMILE!	449-12806-7	$3.99
___STAY!	449-14813-0	$3.99
___THROUGH THE YEAR WITH THE FAMILY CIRCUS	449-90663-9	$8.00
___WANNA BE SMILED AT?	449-12816-4	$3.50
___WE DIDN'T DO IT!	449-13378-8	$3.99
___WE'RE HOME!	449-12427-4	$3.50
___WHERE DID THE SUMMER GO?	449-12426-6	$3.50
___WHERE'S PJ?	449-12974-8	$3.99
___WHO INVENTED RAIN?	449-12423-1	$3.95

Name_____
Address_____
City_____State_____Zip _____

Please send me the FAWCETT BOOKS I have checked above.
I am enclosing $_____
   plus
Postage & handling* $_____
Sales tax (where applicable) $_____
Total amount enclosed $_____

*Add $2 for the first book and 50¢ for each additional book.

Send check or money order (no cash or CODs) to:
Fawcett Mail Sales, 400 Hahn Road, Westminster, MD 21157.

Prices and numbers subject to change without notice.
Valid in the U.S. only.
All orders subject to availability.   KEANE